café poet

Ray Tyndale started writing poetry and literary fiction in the 1990s when studying for her MA in Creative Writing with Tom Shapcott at the University of Adelaide and has continued to publish all manner of words while gaining her doctorate. There are always women in her writing, although they are rarely young. Ray is multi-skilled and has led many lives, all of which enrich her several books. *Farmwoman* (Wakefield Press) and *Sappho at Sixty* (Picaro Press) are among her latest works, both published in 2007.

Lately she has been working as a café poet at Sarah's Sister's Sustainable Café in Semaphore mainstreet, under the ægis of the national body, Australian Poetry. She lives with her partner and dogs in beachside Semaphore, South Australia.

Also by Ray Tyndale

Sleeping Under a Grand Piano: Ten South Australian Poets, 1999
Friendly Street New Poets Six, 2000
Pastorale, Unbridled Tongues Press, 2004
maiden voyage, Unbridled Tongues Press, 2005
Sappho at Sixty, Picaro Press, 2007
Farmwoman, Wakefield Press, 2007
Reflections, Unbridled Tongues Press, 2012
Homecoming, Unbrideld Tongues Press, 2013

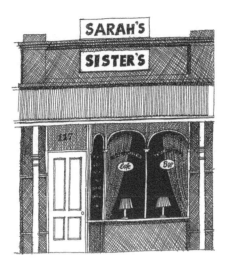

Café Poet

Ray Tyndale

Wakefield
Press

Wakefield Press
1 The Parade West
Kent Town
South Australia 5067
www.wakefieldpress.com.au

First published 2013

Cover image copyright © Stuart Gifford
Typeset by Wakefield Press
Printed in Australia by Griffin Digital, Adelaide

National Library of Australia Cataloguing-in-Publication entry

Author: Tyndale, Ray R. (Ray Rosalind).
Title: Café poet / Ray Tyndale.
ISBN: 978 1 74305 205 1 (pbk.).
Dewey Number: A821.4

**Government
of South Australia**

Arts SA

fox creek
wines

for all at
Sarah's Sister's Sustainable Café
in Semaphore

My thanks to Australian Poetry for the opportunity to be a café poet in the café of my choice. Naturally, my choice was local, vegetarian and completely welcoming.

My thanks to Stuart Gifford and Marion Prosser, owners of the café; to all the friendly staff, and to the many people who enjoy the café, especially those who opened their hearts to me.

I enjoyed many free cups of coffee and lovely snacks, and an outpouring of people's life stories.

It was a great experience.

Contents

on being a café poet

If ever there was a place
where one was going to be a café poet
Sarah's Sister's Sustainable Café
would have to be first choice.

Not full of the literati set
nor any particular set
but regulars from near and far
and drop-ins, tourists and the curious.

Wrapped around by a garden nursery,
café curtains open to the water feature
fountains and flowers
hanging baskets of seasonal colour.

Many browsers in the nursery
mosey on into the café
through the open back door,
sit down to coffee in the sun.

Nearly lunchtime
and waitress Jess is setting
thick white paper napkins,
water glasses and cutlery

and tattered copies of
much re-used menu sheets
which set out the café's values
as well as the food.

Not called Sustainable for nothing,
the food is not recycled but
just about everything else is,
especially the story menus:

four hand-written pages
only two with elaborate food suggestions,
the other two covered top to bottom
with Stuart's Vision.

He only runs a café
because urban design and
pen-and-ink work and painting
don't pay, but don't ever think

he doesn't do *this* job well
because customers come back
from across town for the food
as well as the good feeling.

Sometimes sparrows come down
to dine on tasty pastry crumbs
or risotto fragments. Delicate little feet
hoppity hop to the dark undersides

of tables and chairs.
There's one here now.
Even when the curtains are closed
on cool days they know their way in

escaping through cracks
at the top with crumbs for the nest.
The chooks that roam the nursery
don't come in but scuttle

under the safety of garden benches when
customers get too close,
coming out to crow –
those funny bantams called Silkies,

splayed feet and comic wattles.
The single hen has a bad time
with four roosters but they look
entirely right in the setting.

I find it hard to march
up to strangers and start talking
about poetry but it's amazing
how interested most diners are.

Every now and then I meet
a complete rebuttal.
I know when to butt out
if someone says to me

'I just come in here for a coffee
and a bit of peace and quiet.'
Those warning signals
are easily read.

One diner says to me 'Oh no
I'm not at *all* interested in poetry.'
I am fairly green as a café poet;
back off immediately

somewhat chastened. Later
she comes around looking
at the paintings on the café walls,
a local artist known to her.

Maybe she is acknowledging
her abruptness. She comments
on the beautiful surroundings
which draw her to the garden setting.

'I love a garden' she says
'all that greenery and flowers and stuff
but all I have at home is
tar and cement   just tar and cement'

tar and cement

> just tar and cement
> my backyard
> but I love to see
> sunshine on greenery
> and hear the splash of
> fountain, cluck of hen
>
> why doesn't my backyard
> look like that?

The writing of a tiny little poem
opens her heart.
She weeps a little, folds it in four
and stores it away in her wallet.

When she leaves she asks me
for my card and then I feel
I have a partial convert
to the power of poetry.

when is a street a mainstreet?

'every mainstreet
needs a pub and a church'
well Semaphore Road
certainly qualifies
three pubs and one working
church and one empty
unloved and unsaleable
but what about
the cafés – twenty four
at last count and fast food
outlets – might be ten of those
and for some reason
three chemist shops
we must be a community
of hypochondriacs
or maybe we're overfed

there's a proliferation
of gift shops interspersed
with charity shops
and barbers – two –
but only one hairdresser
Semaphore would seem
to qualify admirably
as a mainstreet

the coffee drinker in Sarah's Sister's
who knows about these things
he's in Place Management
whatever that is
he challenges me when
I talk of Semaphore Mainstreet
but I think I satisfy him
sufficiently perhaps
to take a walk down the street
our mainstreet with
a pub and a church or two

on not sounding Australian

Edinburgh to Adelaide
twenty years now
but both diners broad Scots
a lilting east coast brogue
carrying them through
Greenwich Village and
Beat Poets and Bob Dylan and
outwards to the Great South Land

think about that lilt
which never leaves the Scot
and the taste of the bog
always in the Irish throat
but the English   the English
lose the plum in the mouth
or have it mocked out
another bloody Pom   an epithet
cruel enough to cut the accent dead

The Tuesday Lunch Club

for Nancy, Barbara, Trish, Jan and Peggy

it really doesn't matter
whether the food is sustainable
or not   sustaining the conversation
is what matters
after the concentration of yoga
and the silence of relaxation
the Tuesday Lunch Club talks
well sprinkled with laughter
but also with honesty
about house prices and medications
vegetarianism and vet bills
go-karting and gardening
among other things
beneath the laughter
the great affection
of good friends

forcefeeding

for Trish at Sarah's Sister's

no time to bottle the plums
pack them in syrup
freeze for icecream
plum sauce can come later

ripe tomatoes though
won't wait so
ketchup to the elbows
on my weekend off

plant some more basil
from seeds I've saved
replace the depletion
from the latest batch of pesto

tonight at work
I'll forcefeed a lassie
left in her twenties
in a crash twenty years ago

to make someone eat
who's reluctant
is part of my job
but unpleasant

from farming stock
I love growing food
value the citrus and nuts
fruit and vegetables fresh
and full of vitality

if only the life force
could move
move this young lass
to learn the world in her forties
that would make me happy

bad dog Dave

for Fiona – as lively as Dave

ouch I cried
as bad dog Dave
crashed between my legs
stayed like a saddleless horse
oops, sorry about that
said his owner
whippets smile
did you know?
especially when treats are around
bad dog Dave always knows
whose pockets are full
he's only young
but already has made
a name for himself
on Semaphore beach
bad dog Dave
we all love him
and he knows

the green lady

for Margaret at Sarah's Sister's

alone but not lonely
at work but not weary
soignée but not brassy
quiet but not shy
contented but not complacent
happy

happy when watching life go by
at Sarah's Sister's Sustainable Café
every weekend
sometimes overlooking the garden
sometimes watching the street
life and nature

alone but not lonely

sometimes Sarah's Sister's is full of activists of one kind
or another

Kalyna's loyalty to the Greens

just mine the copper and silver
and leave the uranium in the ground
whadda we want
no uranium
when do we want it   now

it's all spin anyway   hundreds
of jobs and money for SA
no wars   no bombs
no nuclear anything
uranium is an evil rock
its refinement not responsible
whadda we want
nuclear free
when do we want it
now

democracy?

here we have a by-election
in our parliamentary democracy
we get to choose
who we vote for
which is why we listen
to our candidate today
but we don't get to choose
to vote or not
because we have to vote
or else fork out

in Athens
birthplace of democracy
only certain males
got the vote
no equality there

and if a chosen voter
chose not to vote
he wasn't fined
just turfed out of the city
alive if he was lucky

the freedom to vote
is hard fought for
many in the world
fight for it still

for us in our democracy
to vote is often a chore
but is really our chance
to make democracy work for us

how lucky are we?

on the other hand:

we're asked to vote compulsorily
we're told it's democratic
but politics in this country
is getting plutocratic

ruled not so much by wealth
as by companies with clout
ideas of social equity
are definitely out

tolerance and reason
have lost their popularity
minorities and migrants
lead to community polarity

the candidate

amazing the self assurance
of a well-educated youth
able to spring into action
on the political front

a teenager still
feeling his way into the world
he is certain he can
represent an electorate

not just any electorate
but the one he's grown up in
his local   his passion
his home

spin is laughed off
policies quite shaky
but not his resolve
to get into parliament

and uphold democracy:
his definition of that?
good at prevarication
halfway there laddie

youth coalition

the earnestness
of members of a coalition
of young people
to bring about climate change
reminds me of the preacher
on the corner by Scots Church
or of the Goths into Resistance
in the nineties or even
God forbid the *Jugend*
saluting in their uniform

they see themselves
saving the planet
beware the earnestness
of the Nazi police
I am certain
Gaddafi and Mugabe
meant well
when they started out

chook talk

'chook   chook   choooook:
they're not taking
any notice of me
don't they recognise
chook talk?'
the silkie bantam
parades up and down
on her own   peace at last
from her four roosters
time to wander the garden
eat the mosquitos
from the pool
without competition
being by herself
'leave me in peace'
she seems to say
'go cluck somewhere else
please'

a demonstration of the uses of native foods, and the café cooking with them

native foods

the old cocky farmers
used to run off the road
driving with their head
over one shoulder
then go into the local shop
to find out what we'd planted
why couldn't they
just come and ask?

'can't irrigate crops
on the flat there
anyone can tell you that
can't be done'

hasn't been done
they mean but
we *are* doing it
and look – it works

muntries and quandongs
saltbush and wattle seeds
native foods growing
exactly where they should
and plenty of people

at least willing to try
tasting and cooking
and serving up
what sounds like exotic
dishes but they're just
not exotic – they're native
they grow here – they're ours

Fiona's take on Anaïs Nin

'Life shrinks and expands in proportion to one's courage'

in the café Fiona quotes
Anaïs Nin from memory
 'I think she said the world is as big
as you are brave'
I think I like Fiona's take better

some people's worlds are small
not by choice
and their every attempt to break out
into a bigger world
must take huge courage
and often fail

others are born
into a world of opportunity
I am not certain
this ensures their bravery

so is the world of Fiona
big and is she brave?

and mine
how big is my world?

I'm afraid to think of it

Dr WHO?

Fifty years ago
I was exterminated
by a Dalek
just taller than me
at the time

It stuck its wand
in my face
and it said
in Dalek dialect
'EXTERMINATE'
I was so thrilled
I've never forgotten

Now my grandson
has Dalek lego ©
Dalek T-shirts ©

and Dalek
mobile phone cover ©
but he hasn't
met a real one –
not like me

a conversation beside Sarah's Sister's fire
extinguisher – which has a sign: BEWARE DIAL-ECTS

Mary Mary, quite contrary …

I don't want a roll
I want chips
I don't want juice
I want Coke
I don't want cheese
I want Vegemite
I don't want Vegemite
I want cheese
I don't want my coat off
I'm too hot
I don't want a cushion
I want to kneel
I've got pins and needles
I don't want a drink
I want chips
I don't want to behave …

not a Big Mac

the children ponder
the camouflage
the pretense that the burger
is a Big Mac
when in fact
it's deliciously roasted
Mediterranean veggies
covered with sweet
caramelised onions
in a crispy bun
with a beautiful side salad
putting the golden arches
to shame

they're polite
but one can't help thinking
they'd prefer
something a bit more
familiar

misadventure

children   fascinated by water
hang against the ropes
adults watching
out of the corners of their eyes
inevitably   eventually
one of their tiny plastic toys
falls into the water
tears fall   Italian tears
less restrained than Australian
a glumness descends
eyes are rubbed
Papa is called
he can't reach
the gardener turns off
the fountains   the bubbler
the toy is retrieved
well of course it is
tears are dried
ready for the next (mis)adventure

earthing

the theory is
we've lost our connection
with the earth
leading to all these
nasty auto-immune thingies
like eczema and asthma
and multiple sclerosis
so we need to get back onto the ground –
bit hard with ms – down and dirty
sitting on the lawn or the beach
or lying in bed
with a lead attached to the ground
well earthed like a house
against lightning
but this is supposed
to re-wire the brain
charged you might say
all fired up and ready to go
ready for anything
that's the theory

panâche

if you wear
a sufficiently slinky
tight-fitting frock
extra eyelashes
for effect and
stilettos of course

when you get home
staying with Mother
nobody's home   no key
cross-legged
no two ways about it
the catflap
looks very inviting

will you strip
before squeezing?
sure to get stuck
embarrass oneself
and the fireman

so fully dressed
dive in
a lot of wriggle
a new take on
popping in

Bob's jumper

He's wearing a multi-striped
vividly coloured yakwool jumper
the sort that Mike wears beneath
his flowing white hair on Time Team
Bob's jumper came from
the local hippy shop
next to the health store
on Semaphore mainstreet
purchased a very long time ago
and darned at the point of maximum use
right over his stomach
which is full of Stuart's
excellent Mediterranean burger
the darns match the many
colours of the jumper but not the stripes
so the pattern is eye-catching and pretty
not only does this splendid jumper
keep Bob toasty warm
it also brightens the café
and our lives

and for a different Bob:

flutterby

his mind flits like a butterfly
between golf and gardening
music and quotable quotes
The Goon Show and My Music
but no slowing down
for this octogenarian
he's already been shopping
at a Hills farmers' market
before enjoying his usual
morning coffee at the café
on Saturday

proud of his age
as well he may be
many of us will be glad
to have a mind that
flits like a butterfly and lands lightly
when we get to 80

downward dog

for Linda

the yoga teacher /
she's well known in Semaphore /
came to my workplace
not for long enough
so I took my loyalty
back to her classes
eight years ago

such pleasure looking forward
to my weekends
salute to the sun
downward dog
easing the stresses
of office life
battling the politicians
and the irrigators
increasing the salinity
of our precious Murray

seven thousand gigalitres
the scientists say
would keep our river
sweet and flowing
two and a half thousand

is on offer
we should grab it
while we can
better than nothing
which is what
we may end up with

yoga soothes my mind
and body but it seems
nothing will soothe
the river system
too little   too late

snatched lives

for Sue at Sarah's Sister's

not a prisoner in my father's house
but a daughter
not in thrall to my husband
but wife and mother
I went from family home
to empty nest content and complicit
but not myself
divorce showed me this

entirely alone
I set off to explore the whole world
my first choice, Iceland
was wonderful but cold

the Arctic Circle even more so
and Canada and Siberia –
I did choose places as cold
as my home was not

for two years with little baggage
alone I quenched
my thirst for freedom
now I can go wherever I like
and come home
whenever I wish

unsettled

for Cheryl Ann at Sarah's Sister's

teaching's not what it used to be
full of rules and regulations
which are not aimed
at improving learning
but at avoiding
all possibility of
legal action

and as one ages
life becomes more rulebound
much less pleasure
the children are lovely
cheeky and interested
but the departmental rigidity
is unsettling and I forget things
also unsettling

retirement beckons

wounds

for many families
their life together
is a series
of little hurts

hopefully forgiveness
kicks in
wounds heal
hurts forgotten

but for many
something or someone
rubs salt in the wounds
they simmer on

then forgiveness
is hard to give or receive
and the family
is broken forever

restoration

i.m. Edward Lynch, Arkaba Station, 1887

Jill's grandmother
was run over and killed
crossing Torrens Road
at Ovingham

after years of hardship
of widowhood and emigration
bringing up sons and making her way
she had remarried onto Arkaba Station

harsh outback station life
in the days before
transport and telecommunications
then farming in the South East
all that living and loving
to get run over seems so poignant
and sad

Jill's grandfather kept
a little book of prayers
a Catholic meditation
now I am brought this book
to repair with care
the poet turns bookbinder
how good it is to have several strings
to my bow

with infinite care I straighten out
the delicate gold edging
unpick over a hundred years
of mending and sewing
not a seamstress repair
but I imagine it kept
the book in daily use

transparent Japanese paper
replaces corners of pages
gnawed by mice or maybe silverfish
the cover is embossed
complete with cross
but missing its spine
a new spine is going to be obvious
I'll never match
the original brown cover
so not a true restoration

Jill brings me this book
wrapped in tissue paper
and doesn't know
why she keeps it nor for whom
family members not interested
at the moment
doesn't really know
why *she* has inherited it
but feels a need to treasure it
for posterity
or maybe for the memory
of her grandmother
run over crossing the road

Public transport

It's only when you experience
transport systems in other cities
Sydney $2 day tickets
on the buses and trains
right down south to Kiama
and Melbourne trams running
constantly without delay and
right across the city
that you realize
just how inefficient is
the public transport in Adelaide.
There is a city in Europe
where the system works so well
trams buses and trains run
like clockwork without timetables:
imagine that!
Now with an economic downturn
things in Adelaide
will only get worse

play

We dug a tunnel
heading towards the beach
from Newman Street.

We'd watched some war film
about escape: our play
was always exciting,

based on whatever
was on at the local flicks,
but this was serious stuff.

We started under the stables:
the neighbour wondered
why his racehorse was twitchy.

We dug carefully and shored up
with galvo from the tip
all sworn to secrecy.

Digging through sand
dangerous, adrenalin-filled
and hidden.

Buckets of sand secreted
to the beach unnoticed.
We were left to ourselves,

a freedom not enjoyed
by today's children.
Times change.

We got a long way with our tunnel
but never finished,
some other movie pricking

our imagination in another
direction but nobody dobbed.
No one ever knew.

last time I saw you

ah Genevieve
sweet Genevieve
last time I saw you
I thought would be the last time

your face screwed up with pain
staggering on two sticks
quite unable to enjoy life
dependent on your sister
to get about

now look at you
twenty years on
the chiropractor's skill
has given you new life
but the loving sister
has passed on

it is lovely to see you
and unexpected
sharing time with the niece
and little greatniece

outside Sarah's Sister's
meeting and greeting passers-by
an active part
of the community

whoever would have thought ...?

imagine all the people

for Stuart Gifford at Sarah's Sister's

we need dreamers in this mad world
of dirty cities   lack of land to grow food
polluted streams and seas
acid rain   radioactivity
religious wars   forced marriages
the list is endless
we need dreamers

dreamers can envision
global peace and harmony
a John Lennon imagination
for a cool world
enough food for everyone
alternative power   clear air
all the things we don't have

just because we don't have this world
doesn't mean we can't imagine having it
doesn't mean we can't
all acknowledge one Supreme Being
can't re-design our cities for clean living
can't clean up our rivers
re-educate polluters   doesn't mean
we can't grow enough food to feed

all the world's hungry
as well as ourselves

such are the things
that dreams are made of
but governments
need to listen to dreams
grass roots movements
can fire the imagination
but policy-makers
make things happen
or not

the dreamer here at Sarah's Sister's
draws magical plans for
a vertical garden city here in the Port
roof gardens   water taxis
passive solar apartments
with recycled water
cascading down the buildings
feeding vertical farms and
keeping the block cool –
reach out of your window
to pluck a lettuce
or climb the stairs
to dig the vegetable beds
and admire the view
from the roof

dreams are all very well
and drawings are exciting
but how do we make it all happen?
how do we the people
move on from just imagining?

fear

three women share
a huge pot of tea
and gossip
interrupted by the sight
of fluffy white bantams
out in the flower nursery
most people laugh
at the incongruity

one of the women
raises her hands to her cheeks
in horror at the idea
of chickens and feathers and threat

the other women take her seriously
don't laugh at her
on leaving they leave behind
only lipstick marks
on their teacups

implants

for Veronica at Sarah's Sister's

fed up spitting her
lower plate out
at students and guests
Vee decides to go for implants
without reckoning
on psych pain
surprised to discover
memories rushing in
of mouthfuls of blood
and powerlessness
at thirteen

a violent father had knocked out
her two front teeth
might as well
agreed mother and dentist
rip 'em all out
while the going's good
so the young girl
ate pap for six weeks
and learnt early
to manage false teeth

now nearing fifty
embarrassed by her plates
unable to remove them
at night before her lover
wary of smiling
she prepares herself
for a mouthful of implants
and many more weeks
of pap

after huge expense
she will now have to learn
to clean her teeth
but the smile will be worth it
she hopes

gossip

Is gossip a gender thing?
What do men do
when they hang out together
at the pub or
around the barbie?
Talk sport or work or family?
Talk to hurt themselves and others

or is this where
talkback radio comes in?
Men's gossip sessions.
Thinking of Alan Jones et al
these sessions are often
poisonous and very public
whereas women's gossip

is usually less public
although often vituperative
but between the gossipers only,
not on air, and often

full of ideas and helpful
suggestions. The women
at the table next to me
have finished discussing

dysfunctional relationships
and are now talking
art and fashion and babies:
things that excite them.

So much better. They'll
go home feeling brighter
having got things
off their chests.
Does this happen for men?

lovers

he kisses her
he kisses her again and again
their heads together
as they murmur

they have moved their chairs
side by side at the table
oblivious to the crowded
café, to the steady rain
in the garden nursery
oblivious to everything
but themselves

brought coffee and cake
they eat ravenously
the hunger of sex

a final kiss and they're off

From Helen's use of the verb *to catastrophise*

catastrophising lover:
he's not answering
his mobile
he must have been
in an accident
in hospital
he must be dead

illustration

talking to the Elizabeths at Sarah's Sister's

she gets all tartened up
to dance with her Scottish mates
with a name like Munro
there's an expectation there
even if it's just
her married name

I love Scottish dancing
but can't do it any more
and I'm envious
oh says her mother
(also called Elizabeth)
you can watch
nothing more frustrating
than sitting out
while others dance

Elizabeth illustrates her own poems
the sketching more important
than the words maybe
although with 800 poems
under her belt
she takes it seriously

they're only about
everyday things she demurs
but I – naturally –
think those are the most important
things in the world

beards

they're back in fashion
says the bearded man
as I count the faces
turned towards the camera
ten men and eight of them
sporting bristles above and below
the mouth but many of them
are thinning on top
to varying degrees

do their beards make up
for the baldness or is
the baldness the result
of too much
follicle chin growth?

the two beardless men
don't have much hair
on their heads either
so that theory is blown
but they do in fact
look a little less manly

I'd go for beards
personally

buy a pie shop to mend
a broken heart

Mrs Penrice's pie shop
no longer in Semaphore Road
pushed out by the café strip
no room for three bakeries
in one shopping street

the original Mrs Penrice
– lovely Cornish name –
lived in the Big White House
and started cooking at home
pies and pasties – Cornish of course

soon custom built up
a new shop opened
opposite her house
handy for the cinema
became very popular

franchises opened
up and down the coast
and soon Mrs Penrice
could retire on the proceeds

Lee bought her out
now Lee was a hairdresser
a broken-hearted beautician

looking for a change
so pies and pasties with ketchup
or real tatty oggies*
occupied her full-time
drove a stake through heartache
long enough to set up
another breakable relationship
I am a bandaid says Lee
ruefully

later she took her bandaid skills
to greater heights after the pie shop
with a women's support group
and fund-raising for all sorts of
cut-up-rough clients
in dire need of bandaids

her remedies are of no use
to her own broken heart
skewered yet again
he went off to America
with an internet lover
who tickled his ear
with more than anything
she had to offer

back in Semaphore
she seeks solace in Sarah's Sister's
but all she finds is me

* *tatty oggies: the real thing, never called a Cornish pasty in
   Cornwall*

High Tea

So what is everyone expecting
for High Tea?
such a pretentious name
in a laid-back arty sort of
café like Sarah's Sister's
just not Australian

Afternoon Tea in England
conjures cucumber sandwiches
or at the very least little
triangles of bread and butter
followed by small iced cakes
washed down with Twinings
from the pot of course
not a teabag in sight

Devonshire teas are delectable:
sometimes scones and jam and
thick clotted cream but also
sometimes a sweet bun
cut nearly in half
filled with raspberry jam
– no other jam will do –
and lashings of cream

High Tea for me
I'm in Scotland and
it's the meal we call dinner
or even supper or just tea
rarely eaten before 6
so this one
at late lunch
is a wee bit early
a raised pork pie perhaps?
loaf-style and sliced in squares
with a lettuce leaf or two
or Scotch eggs of course
or kippers perhaps, an Arbroath smokie
served with a lump
of melting butter and proper
fish knives and forks
maybe a pound cake or
a clootie dumpling after
but only the English
would serve it with custard

So which has it been,
your High Tea?
English, cream or Scots
or thoroughly Australian?
Not, I hope,
a dog's breakfast!

High tea served to ten nurses from the RAH

Semaphore Shorts – haiku

he plucks ideas
as a beachcomber
imagines uses for flotsam

bantam roosters
raucous and repetitive
pretence of importance

scarlet geraniums
not flashing danger
just warm summer pleasure

hot soup
fragrancy curls
body and soul warmed and resuscitated

conversation buzz
gossip flows unchecked
interconnection renewed

winter beach bright sunshine
sastrugi sandblast
surf tossed by biting wind

E.G. is a local, a regular at Sarah's Sister's. She is in her late eighties, and agreed to talk to me about her life.

The following poem is my version of her oral history, put before the reader with her permission.

All names have been changed for confidentiality.

Call me Mimi

Cut the accent with a knife
not broad Geordie
but a lovely soft middle-class
Tyneside lilt   unmistakeable

so familiar to me
my parents had it
grandparents uncles and aunts
even my sister can turn it on

when visiting relatives
but Mimi
sitting dining alone
talking only to the waiter

was an immediate attraction.
With oral history bells ringing
in my head I approached
almost in familiarity

wanting to say
where're you from, bonny lass?
but much more circumspect
much more polite.

Well! I needn't have worried
here was a lady –
certainly not to be claimed
as 'woman' – ready to talk.

Now I look forward
to our conversations
a bit one-sided admittedly
but I can edge in

nudge the flowing stream
in the right direction
bit by bit I'm getting
the whole life story

just exactly what I want!
Right from birth and childhood
in the same suburb of
Gateshead as my mother:

Lowfell, posher than some
suburbs of Newcastle but still
grimy row houses with
the lavatory down the back

the coal-hole alongside
back gate straight onto the lane
immaculate well-scrubbed
front doorstep onto the pavement

with only a tiny strip
of dusty garden – coal dust
and shipyard steel settling
on every single object

even Saltwell Park
with its lake and ducks
dirty but good for play
we're talking 1920s

so no doubt it's much changed.
Mimi was born in 1925.
It's hard to believe this
elegant, soignée lady

is 87, tall and slender,
all in white except the
perfect nails, pale pink;
even the glasses are white.

When she leaves after
our first conversation,
just breaking the ice,
I see she's wearing

high heels to accentuate
her regal height and
no tottering: this is
one amazing lady.

second meeting

just soup and white wine
I only ever have soup
but it saves on electricity
and things going off in the fridge

Today she's still in white
but a turban replaces
the wide-brimmed sunhat.
She tells me her hair is long

tucked on top of her head
only cut once in a lifetime
my husband married me
for my hair   he 14 years dead.

Where were we, she asks
In childhood, I reply
but not for long as soon
she's through school –

that happened in the '30s –
and starting work already.
Her mother – a widow too soon –
worked in the Workhouse

the very name of which conjures up
my own grandmother's terror
that she, also a widow,
would end up there

the shame the indignity
so that hospitalisation at the end
of more than nine decades
was fought like a cat:

for her it was still the Workhouse.
Mimi insists when her mother
worked there it was clean
and comfortable, men and women

separate and a foundling
hospital too for babes
left on the doorstep –
a lovely place to work.

At 15 Mimi went to work
as a 'lady tracer' at
Armstrongs' Rolls Royce factory
but not on the factory floor

oh no! and no co-mingling
with the (male) workers
not even permitted
to look at the men.

After the war she changed
jobs (probably the men
came back from the war)
worked in a Newcastle office

until leaping with enthusiasm
into live-in nannying
in Gosforth in a 'better'
suburb of Newcastle.

The nanny job
is passed over quite quickly
although I sense she
enjoyed it well enough

Went on a holiday 'down south'
with the family to
Kingston-upon-Thames
a totally different milieu.

A new life a new freedom
opened up with swimming
and parties and pubbing
and men!

The holiday never ended
for Mimi who met her
future husband. Nannying
no longer so attractive.

The new man in her life
was an undergrad at Oxford
no marrying until he finished
as his mother had scrimped

to send him there and anyway
one didn't hurry things
in those days
but she did move to Oxford.

His first teaching appointment
was at Woodchester Park
in the Cotswolds with new home
part of a lovely country house

(there are times when Mimi
is quite particular to stress
a class position – so important
in 1940's England

not yet owning a home
but living in comfortable
almost posh surrounds
important to her sense of self).

third meeting

Still all in white
rings on her fingers
reminding her of special
people   special events

but the turban has been
relaced again by the sunhat
which is a better look
but I wouldn't dream of saying

Woodchester, I prompt as
she tucks into her lentil soup
Woodchester Park, she graciously
corrects me, the Park adding

to their position in society
really important   really
important and throughout
our conversations

place in society is gently
stressed again and again.
Houses have been left
jobs deserted in order

to keep up the image
the rightful place
even in Australia
our so-called classless society.

Mimi talks of her married life
in terms of her husband's
career and abilities
rather than her own.

Every move they made
across more than 50 years together
couched in terms
of his scholarship

He was a scholar she reiterates
and I recall she left school
at 15 *I was the practical one*
like chalk and cheese we were

her pride in him palpable
and her married life devoted
to his progress and one could think
she sublimated herself but I think

that would be quite wrong:
his satisfaction in life
was her contentment and fulfilment;
she worked hard at it.

Chislehurst in Kent was a step
upwards with Herbert's own school
for overseas students – English
classes, not like TESOL,

with students grabbing at the chance
to settle in a new country –
but more like a finishing school
for young Europeans

from affluent backgrounds
just touching up their accent
learning about cricket
horse racing and social niceties.

All very well but getting teachers
of suitable character and
capabilities was almost
impossible and the final

three masters were a drunkard
a madman and a child molester –
time for a change –
emigration called!

In 1959 the Education Department
of South Australia was short
of teachers and advertising
in glowing terms in Britain.

Herbert and Mimi fell for it
at a time when England
was still fighting its way
out of post-war penury.

Sunshine and good wages
appreciation of ability,
one has to say promises of
greener pastures come to mind.

After a first class sea voyage
round South Africa (after Suez)
stopping at exotic places
they arrived in Adelaide.

Here is this married English couple
he a scholar and researcher
accustomed to comfort and security
she a loving wife

ready to bring a cultured
gentility to Adelaide children
and where are they placed?
Minlaton, right in the middle

of the wastes of Yorke Peninsula
terrible housing   terrible flies
barbecues and beer and footy
an alien culture

quite removed from anything
in their imagination
in the Land of Promise;
they lasted six months.

He was a scholar you see
lesser men would have been broken
but he had the backing
of a determined woman.

Back to Adelaide they went;
he took a position teaching
in a private college before
a Melbourne research job turned up.

Melbourne in the early '60s
was more genteel even than Adelaide
more conducive to a quiet
cultured family life.

fourth meeting

Each time we meet
there's some back-tracking to do
and also Mimi needs to get
some pet grouse off her chest

living alone for fourteen years
outliving most of her friends
she's lonely and welcomes
the chance to be listened to.

For a start today she talks
of her husband's degrees
each time he changed jobs, she says
he would take another degree

again the laugh *oh ho* becoming
more the scholar with each one
while Mimi continues to be
thoroughly practical, alone.

This time our meeting
is coloured by pamphlets dug out
of the large white handbag and handed
to me nonchalantly, as though

unimportant but in reality
critical to her memory
of elegance and comfort
at Woodchester Park

all those years ago
at the beginning of marriage
and home-making.
Foreign students stayed

to perfect their English;
Mimi cooked and cleaned and
perfected her gentility
but enjoyed the students.

The brochure of Woodchester 'Mansion'
shows an unfinished
Victorian pile, unfinished
but very impressive

set in a quiet Cotswold
valley with woodland and
lake and a long walk from the road
a mile and a half away.

Must have been an amazing place
to start married life!
Herbert does his teaching certificate
and practise in Leicester while

Mimi stays put and cooks and cleans
until mother-in-law takes pity
on her loneliness and she moves
in with her in Barrow-in-Furness.

Did Mimi complain of her loneliness?
I doubt it, anymore than she does now.
Bucket-loads of stiff upper lip
and backbone, even then.

This diploma of Herbert's
was precursor to opening
his own school for foreign students
in a large house, purchased

in partnership with his brother,
in Chislehurst in Kent:
other end of the country
but closer to Europe

and the supply of students
although many came from
Pakistan and Persia and
Other Exotic Places.

Our fourth meeting
over leek and potato soup
side-tracks into familial
relationships, divorces

misdemeanours and misadventures
which need not bother us here
although every now and then
something tickles her fancy

and Mimi's tinkling laughter
rings out across the café;
very hard not to be amused
at the, sometimes wicked gossip.

fifth meeting

I was forty when I had
my daughter Emma;
thought it was never going to happen
and she was the only one.

Herbert was off at work
researching for the Education Dept
I was happy to homemake
                    and childrear

which I did very well, I think,
and Emma is a credit
to us and has
her father's brains.
The laughter tinkles out again.

What has amused her so?
I wonder but laughter
often covers confusion
or pain and how will
I know and she will not say.

This fifth meeting
Mimi comes in navy
but white underneath
and still the high heels

with gold lace sockettes
to protect her toes
if I can't wear heels
I won't go out she says

but the nails are not perfect
two are missing
the beautician is in hospital
and Mimi reveals two bitten nails.

Her embarrassment is tangible
but I knew they weren't real
they were just too perfect
but fit the image.

It is so hard
to get Mimi to talk
about her own life
he was a scholar

reiterated over and over
and *chalk and cheese*
without ever making the point
she was the practical one

the essential cog in
the machine of their life together
again and again I try
to bring her back to herself

but she slips out from under
again and again and I hear
another story about another
brother-in-law or uncle

aunts or nephews even
and the grandson she brought up
herself while daughter Emma
suffered following the birth.

I hear about the grandson
and the second grandson
but still I don't hear
about herself.

Like so many women
of her generation
she had subsumed herself
entirely in her husband

and he's been dead
for fourteen years
And these last fourteen years?
Not important.

sixth meeting

Here is this feisty woman
fourteen years a widow
but running her life
exactly as she likes.

She avoids other nationalities
scorns feminism and is more
than a little homophobic
but charming in spite of it

and laughing at herself:
that tinkling laugh makes it hard
to be critical and I'm sure she's unaware
of any offence she may give.

seventh meeting armed with questions

This time I'm determined
not to be sidetracked
but once I get some answers
Mimi steers the conversation

once more away from
her own life – not
in the least bit interesting to her
though fascinating to me.

In the seventies when
Herbert transferred back
to Adelaide University
then the Examinations Board

there was an awful lot of
moving house for one reason
or another and the complete
building of two new houses.

There always seemed a particular
reason for each move
house too small or too big
wrong suburbs or neighbours

and one house that
fell down a cliff (after
it was sold, poor buyers).
Another to be on the flat

for a husband by now
struck down with a disease
not unlike Parkinson's
that meant he fell a lot.

Heathpool, Magill, Somerton Park
by now the daughter is a teenager
Kingston Park to make room
for a study then on

to Hallett Cove for grandmother
duties and voluntary jobs
and entertaining Mimi's sister
out from England

three years in a row.
This is the first time Mimi
has talked about her sister
six years her senior so

ten years old when mother
was left a widow,
perhaps a more difficult age to be
left fatherless than Mimi's four.

but the sister must have
enjoyed South Australia
getting to know her baby sister
three years in a row

It was this house at Hallett Cove
that fell down the cliff
three months after they moved.
Mimi's laugh echoes out

right across the café
I can laugh at anything
she says – even other's misfortune
as well as her own.

Suddenly she veers off
to a memory of the Armstrong Siddeley
tracer's office and a comment
from a man to a young Mimi

quite innocent but with
hindsight recognising his
quote of the hymn 'Lead
Kindly Light' was not without

deeper meaning as the
next line is *'amid the encircling gloom*
lead thou me on'
she laughs at the memory

happy for me to understand
that she was not without
'gentlemen admirers' or worldly
experience before marriage.

subsequent meetings

I realise now as I sit talking to Mimi
that in a sense I've milked
her dry and now all that remains
are memories. She's tired

of being asked about her youth
or her marriage or child-rearing
except for flashes of events long ago
that make her laugh when she recalls
them

She'd much rather
talk about now and show me
photos of her two grandsons
and the friends she made

when she went on a cruise last year.
I have to bite my tongue
when she laughs about our
current prime minister:

no feminist rallying there!
And her anger still burns strong
about the treatment of her Presbyterian
Church and its seeming theft,

to her, of all its values
as well as its valuables when
taken over by another denomination.
Old wrongs are not forgiven.

But that's Mimi.
Fight the good fight etc
but always in defence
of those she loves

the lost church
the deceased scholar
the blind friend
the brainy daughter

and through it all she sails
in her beautiful hats
with her manicured nails
and her Italian leather high heels.

Nine decades
of a life well lived.
'Yes, they call me Mimi ...
I'm content and happy'*

* *from Puccini's opera* La Bohéme